OPPONENTS IN AMERICAN HISTORY

SUFFRAGISTS AND THOSE WHO OPPOSED THEM

AMANDA VINK

PowerKiDS press.
New York

Published in 2020 by The Rosen Publishing Group, Inc.
29 East 21st Street, New York, NY 10010

First Edition

Editor: Jane Katirgis
Book Design: Tanya Dellaccio

Photo Credits: Cover (left), pp. 15 (Sojourner Truth), 19, 29 Bettmann/Getty Images; cover (right), p. 13 (The First Convention) Universal History Archive/Universal Images Group/Getty Images; p. 5 Paul Thompson/Hulton Archive/Getty Images; p. 6 https://upload.wikimedia.org/wikipedia/commons/f/fb/Rivista_suffragette.tif; p. 7 (top) https://upload.wikimedia.org/wikipedia/commons/9/92/Annie_Kenney_and_Christabel_Pankhurst_%28cropped%29.jpg; pp. 7 (bottom), 21 (top) Hulton Archive/Getty Images; pp. 9, 13 (Elizabeth Cady Stanton) Everett Historical/Shutterstock.com; p. 11 (Alice Blackwell) Historical/Corbis Historical/Getty Images; pp. 11 (cartoon), 23 Courtesy of the Library of Congress; p. 15 (cartoon) https://upload.wikimedia.org/wikipedia/commons/d/df/Anti-suffrage_postcard-_While_in_the_act_of_voting.jpg; pp. 17, 27 (campaign leaflet) Ken Florey Suffrage Collection/Gado/Archive Photos/Getty Images; p. 21 (bottom) https://upload.wikimedia.org/wikipedia/commons/a/a6/Mayer-Awakening-1915.jpg; p. 25 (Alice Paul) https://upload.wikimedia.org/wikipedia/commons/5/5e/Alice_Paul_%281915%29_by_Harris_%26_Ewing.jpg; p. 25 (procession program) https://upload.wikimedia.org/wikipedia/commons/9/91/Official_program_-_Woman_suffrage_procession_March_3%2C_1913_-_crop.jpg; p. 27 (Woodrow Wilson) Stock Montage/Archive Photos/Getty Images; p. 30 DOMINICK REUTER/AFP/Getty Images.

Cataloging-in-Publication Data

Names: Vink, Amanda.
Title: Suffragists and those who opposed them / Amanda Vink.
Description: New York : PowerKids Press, 2019. | Series: Opponents in American history | Includes glossary and index.
Identifiers: ISBN 9781538345481 (pbk.) | ISBN 9781538343715 (library bound) | ISBN 9781538345498 (6pack)
Subjects: LCSH: Women–Suffrage—United States—History—Juvenile literature. | Suffragists—United States—History—Juvenile literature. | Women's rights—United States—History—Juvenile literature.
Classification: LCC JK1898.V56 2019 | DDC 324.6'23'0973—dc23

Manufactured in the United States of America

CPSIA Compliance Information: Batch #CSPK19. For Further Information contact Rosen Publishing, New York, New York at 1-800-237-9932

CONTENTS

WHO WERE THE SUFFRAGISTS?

On March 3, 1913, more than 5,000 women arrived in Washington, D.C. It was one day before the presidential **inauguration** of Woodrow Wilson. These women, and some men, came to demand women's suffrage, or the right to vote. Two years later, in 1915, about 40,000 people marched the streets of New York City in a parade for the same cause. The fight for women's rights had been growing since the 1800s with much opposition—and it wasn't close to being over. It still continues today.

The women who risked their reputations and often their lives for the right to vote during the 1800s and 1900s came to be known as suffragists. Their voices finally led the U.S. government to give women an equal vote.

IN 1915, ABOUT 40,000 PEOPLE MARCHED THE STREETS OF NEW YORK CITY TO SUPPORT WOMEN'S SUFFRAGE. HOWEVER, ONLY WEEKS LATER, A VOTE TO ALLOW NEW YORK WOMEN SUFFRAGE FAILED. THE FIGHT CONTINUED.

A MOVEMENT FROM ENGLAND

Across the Atlantic Ocean in England, women had been fighting a hard battle for their rights since the early 1800s. The law at that time was that a woman's property transferred to her husband when they married. Women also didn't have the right to vote or to be elected into **Parliament**.

In 1905, Christabel Pankhurst and Annie Kenney of the Women's Social and Political Union (WSPU) interrupted an election rally. They were arrested. Rather than paying a fine, they chose to serve time in jail. Soon after, the *Daily Mail* newspaper referred to women who used more extreme **tactics** as "suffragettes," a play on the term "suffragist." The members of the WSPU took the **derogatory** word and used it to their advantage: they named their journal *The Suffragette*.

The Suffragette

THE PRESS

THE FORCES OF EVIL DENOUNCING THE BEARERS OF LIGHT.

HEAD TO HEAD

The word "male" wasn't used in the U.S. Constitution until the 14th Amendment was ratified, or approved, in 1868.

CHRISTABEL PANKHURST FOUNDED THE WOMEN'S SOCIAL AND POLITICAL UNION WITH HER MOTHER IN 1903.

ARGUMENTS AGAINST SUFFRAGE

Not everyone in England or the United States believed in giving women the right to vote. The reasons for their opposition were numerous. Some people believed that a woman's place was in private. They believed a woman's job was to raise children, manage the home, and be involved with community charities.

One notable woman opposed to women's suffrage was Josephine Jewell Dodge, founder of a charitable day care for working women and the president of the National Federation of Day Nurseries. Dodge believed that giving women the right to vote would take away from charitable organizations and that women would use their talents to support **partisan** causes rather than supporting helpful organizations. Many people believed that politics were dangerous—full of lies and **corruption**—and they feared for women.

THIS CAMPAIGN POSTER SHOWS ONE OF THE POPULAR ARGUMENTS AGAINST SUFFRAGE: THE CLAIM THAT MOST WOMEN DIDN'T WANT TO VOTE.

HEAD TO HEAD

Josephine Jewell Dodge believed men and women were better suited to different roles, or parts, in society. She wrote that it is a "woman's right to be [free] from political responsibility" so that she can offer her best service to the state doing things based on "her nature and her training."

MORE OPPOSITION

Others believed giving women the right to vote was a waste of the country's resources. They argued it would double the cost of elections while not changing the outcome of the vote. Most people assumed women would vote as their husbands did. Those who thought women might vote differently thought that was even more dangerous—that conflicting political views would bring disorder to a home.

In 1909, the *New York Times* reported that Mrs. William Force Scott said, "If women should vote, they must join one of the existing political parties or form a new party of their own—a Woman's Party—and that would be women against men, and more dangerous." Both men and women alike held these viewpoints, and their passionate arguments stretched across a century.

BLACKWELL'S RESPONSE

Debates raged between suffragists and antisuffragists. When antisuffragists argued giving women the right to vote would be costly, Alice Stone Blackwell responded. She wrote, "Women pay their full quota [amount] of the taxes out of which election expenses are paid, and they have been doing this for generations without being permitted to receive any personal benefit from the taxes so applied."

THIS POLITICAL CARTOON SHOWS ANOTHER POPULAR ARGUMENT AGAINST WOMEN'S SUFFRAGE: THE CLAIM THAT WOMEN DIDN'T HAVE THE MENTAL AND EMOTIONAL STRENGTH FOR PUBLIC LIFE.

ALICE STONE BLACKWELL

THE SENECA FALLS CONVENTION

On July 19 and 20, 1848, the first women's rights convention was held in Seneca Falls, New York. Elizabeth Cady Stanton and Lucretia Mott organized the convention. Stanton and Mott were already active players in reform. Stanton had created **petitions** that helped pass a New York bill granting married women's property rights. Mott had been the president of the Philadelphia Female Anti-Slavery Society, although she had been denied recognition at the 1840 World's Anti-Slavery Convention in London, England.

Stanton wrote a Declaration of Sentiments for the Seneca Falls Convention. This statement was based on the Declaration of Independence but highlighted the rights sought by women. Sixty-eight women and thirty-two men signed the declaration. This convention is often considered the start of the U.S. women's suffrage movement.

HEAD TO HEAD

About 300 people attended the Seneca Falls Convention. Two weeks later, some of the attendees met again at the First Unitarian Church of Rochester, New York, to speak with a larger crowd.

ELIZABETH CADY STANTON WAS A TALENTED WRITER AND EDITOR. SHE INCLUDED WOMEN'S RIGHT TO VOTE IN A LIST OF RESOLUTIONS IN HER DECLARATION. THIS RESOLUTION BARELY PASSED.

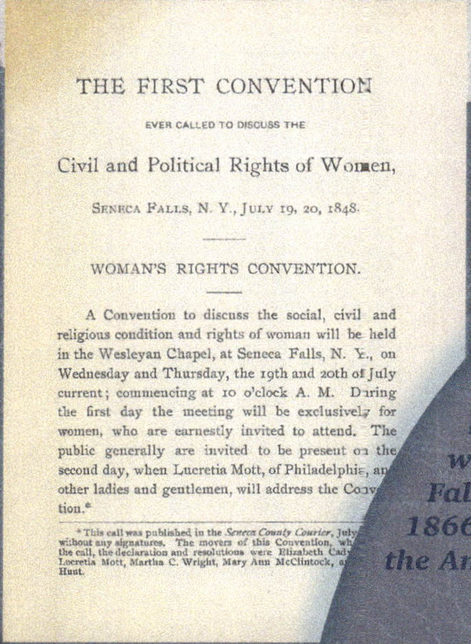

THE FIRST CONVENTION

EVER CALLED TO DISCUSS THE

Civil and Political Rights of Women,

SENECA FALLS, N. Y., JULY 19, 20, 1848.

WOMAN'S RIGHTS CONVENTION.

A Convention to discuss the social, civil and religious condition and rights of woman will be held in the Wesleyan Chapel, at Seneca Falls, N. Y., on Wednesday and Thursday, the 19th and 20th of July current; commencing at 10 o'clock A. M. During the first day the meeting will be exclusively for women, who are earnestly invited to attend. The public generally are invited to be present on the second day, when Lucretia Mott, of Philadelphia, an other ladies and gentlemen, will address the Conv tion.*

* This call was published in the *Seneca County Courier*, July without any signatures. The movers of this Convention, wh the call, the declaration and resolutions were Elizabeth Cady Lucretia Mott, Martha C. Wright, Mary Ann McClintock, a Hunt.

AN ALLY

Former slave and abolitionist Frederick Douglass is most known for his stance against slavery, but when Elizabeth Cady Stanton was criticized for her Declaration of Sentiments, he defended her. Douglass, an ally, or supporter, of the women's suffrage movement, attended the Seneca Falls Convention and signed the declaration. In 1866, he, Stanton, and Susan B. Anthony founded the American Equal Rights Association.

THE MOB CONVENTION

In September 1853, a women's rights convention took place in New York City. About 3,000 people attended. The meeting wasn't a success, as **hecklers** interrupted the speeches and the police didn't try to stop them. In addition, three of New York City's main newspapers made fun of those seeking women's suffrage. This was the first large public **demonstration** against women's suffrage.

Dr. H. K. Root spoke out against women's suffrage using the Christian Bible. Referring to the tale of Adam and Eve in the book of Genesis, Root argued, "The original cause of sin was because man gave up his judgment to woman; and it may be, if we now give up our rights to woman, some great **calamity** may fall upon us."

SOJOURNER TRUTH

A former slave, Sojourner Truth spoke out for abolition, ***temperance****, civil rights, and women's rights. She attended the so-called mob convention, and because she was both an African American and a woman, she was* ***ridiculed*** *even more. Still, she continued, saying, "You may hiss as much as you like, like any other lot of geese, but you can't stop it; it's bound to come."*

ANTISUFFRAGIST POSTCARDS LIKE THIS ONE SOMETIMES MADE IT DIFFICULT FOR SUFFRAGISTS TO GATHER SUPPORT.

SOJOURNER TRUTH

THE FIRST STATE

In 1869, the territory of Wyoming granted women the right to vote and to hold public office. Other territories began to do the same. The Utah territorial government granted the right to vote to women in 1870, but this was reversed by the United States Congress in 1887.

When Wyoming was admitted to the United States as a state in 1890, it was the first state to have women's suffrage. In Colorado, voters approved women's suffrage in 1893. A number of territories and states followed, including Idaho, Washington, and California. In 1913, Illinois gave women the vote, becoming the first state east of the Mississippi River to do so. Some people argue that the West was more willing to give women the vote because women played a critical role in settling the territories.

STATES APPROVED WOMEN'S SUFFRAGE AT DIFFERENT POINTS IN TIME. THIS CARD ENCOURAGED VOTERS TO PRESS THE ISSUE IN NEW YORK STATE.

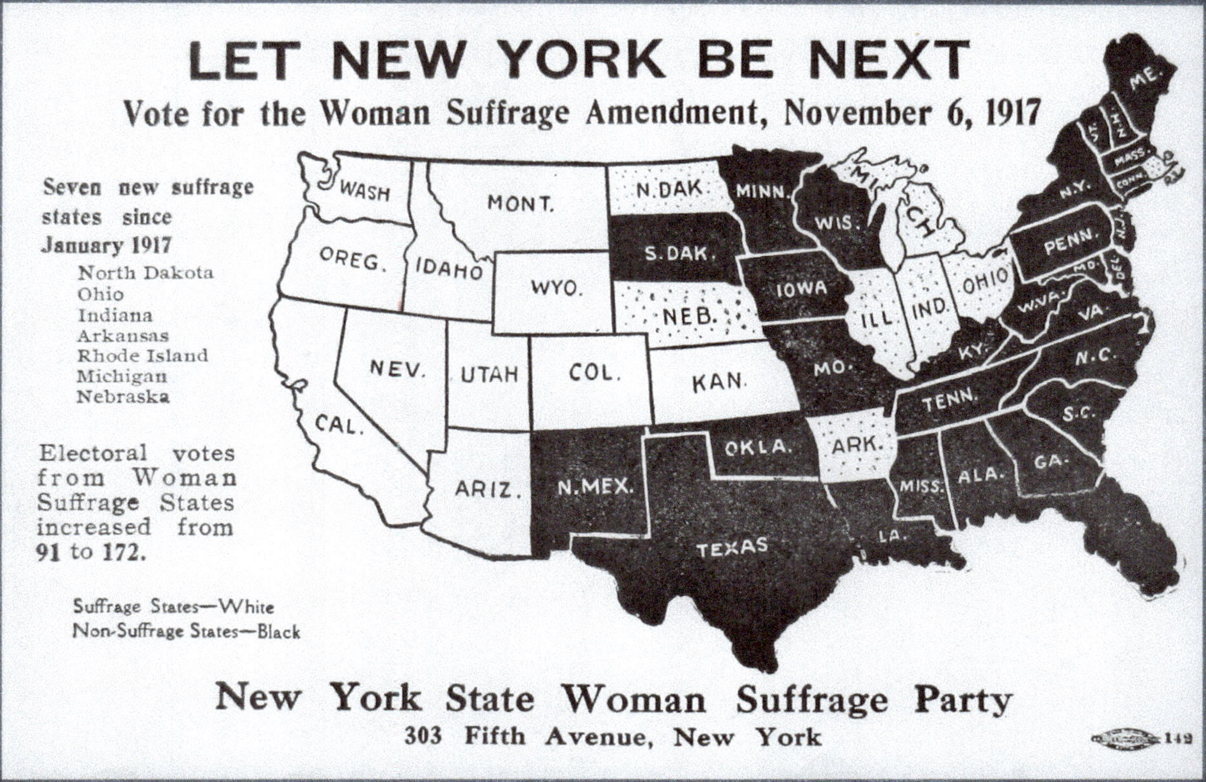

FLIP-FLOPPING ON SUFFRAGE

Some people didn't like the Mormon religion, in part because some Mormons practiced polygamy, allowing men to have more than one wife at the same time. Mormons had founded the Utah territory. Some people thought Utah women's right to vote would favor the Mormon religion, so the U.S. Congress passed a law that reversed the decision. In 1896, when Utah became a state, its new constitution gave women the right to vote again.

FRACTURES

Even within the women's suffrage movement, there were differing opinions. In 1869, the movement split into two groups. Elizabeth Cady Stanton and Susan B. Anthony founded the National Woman Suffrage Association (NWSA) while Lucy Stone, Henry Blackwell, Julia Ward Howe, and others formed the American Woman Suffrage Association (AWSA).

The NWSA wanted to push for a constitutional amendment, which would affect all of the United States at once. The AWSA wanted to target states individually, as members believed it was a more **attainable** goal. The two organizations merged in 1890 and formed the National American Woman Suffrage Association (NAWSA) with a combined goal: to get enough states to approve women's suffrage to force Congress to approve an amendment.

THE 15TH AMENDMENT

In 1870, the 15th Amendment gave black men the right to vote. While many of the women involved with the women's rights movement, including Stanton and Anthony, had worked for abolition, they didn't support the amendment because they wanted an amendment for universal suffrage. Others did support it. This split is one of the reasons the NWSA and the AWSA formed.

SUSAN B. ANTHONY WAS ONE OF THE FOUNDERS OF THE NATIONAL WOMAN SUFFRAGE ASSOCIATION. IN 1872, SHE WAS ARRESTED FOR ILLEGALLY VOTING IN THE PRESIDENTIAL ELECTION.

THE PROGRESSIVE ERA

Over time, more and more states began to support votes for women. The world was changing as more women began to get involved in different campaigns. The Progressive Era was a period from about 1890 through 1920 when social **activism** and reform became very important. Reformers opened libraries and other public buildings, cared for orphans and the children of working families, and provided food for the hungry.

While many progressives were actively against woman's suffrage, the charitable work inspired many women to take an active role in politics and social campaigns—and it would be easier to effect political change once women were allowed to participate in politics. The women's movement was greatly affected by the Progressive Era.

THE PROGRESSIVE ERA BETWEEN THE 1890s AND THE 1920s SAW A RAPID INCREASE IN SOCIAL REFORM, INCLUDING GROWING SUPPORT FOR WOMEN'S RIGHTS.

OPPOSED TO WOMEN'S SUFFRAGE

In 1911, a group of women founded the National Association Opposed to Woman Suffrage (NAOWS). Many antisuffrage organizations had been well established in individual states. This new organization was intended to be a national response to the growing suffragist movement. Josephine Jewell Dodge was one of the founders of the group.

In 1913, the Washington, D.C., office of NAOWS was located only a block away from the office of the congressional committee of NAWSA, where Alice Paul, Lucy Burns, and others were fighting for suffrage. What resulted was a campaigning war. Each side targeted the efforts of the other. The campaign against the suffragists included representations of women who were unattractive, unmarried, older, or very young and overly innocent. In turn, the suffragists targeted the "Antis" with similar tactics.

ONLOOKERS READ FLYERS IN THE WINDOW OF THE HEADQUARTERS OF THE NATIONAL ASSOCIATION OPPOSED TO WOMAN SUFFRAGE, AN ORGANIZATION MEANT TO BLOCK WOMEN FROM SUFFRAGE ON A NATIONAL LEVEL.

HEADQUARTERS NATIONAL ASSOCIATION
OPPOSED TO
WOMAN SUFFRAGE

RADICAL SUFFRAGETTES

While the campaign continued, it seemed the rate of progress was at a slow crawl. Some suffragists began to use more **radical** methods. Alice Paul started the National Woman's Party (NWP) and brought tactics used by the suffragettes of England to the United States. Members began to picket the White House, which means they marched and stood outside with signs. Many of these protesters were arrested.

Arrested suffragists were often treated very badly—especially one day that came to be known as the "Night of Terror." On November 15, 1917, guards beat and injured a number of suffragists in a Virginia prison. News of this "Night of Terror" helped gain public support for the movement. Some women, including Paul, also began hunger strikes—and they were force-fed with tubes down their throats.

ALICE PAUL

IN ADDITION TO PROTESTING AT THE WHITE HOUSE, ALICE PAUL ORGANIZED MARCHES AND RALLIES TO PROMOTE EQUALITY FOR WOMEN. PAUL WAS JAILED SIX TIMES BEFORE THE 19TH AMENDMENT BECAME LAW.

WOODROW WILSON SPEAKS OUT

During his first term, President Woodrow Wilson had a more limited stance for women's suffrage: he supported it at the state level but didn't push for a national amendment. Many women were angry about this, and the picketing outside the White House directly targeted the president.

The protesting had an effect: by 1918, the House of Representatives had approved the 19th Amendment, which would give all U.S. women the right to vote. However, the Senate had yet to vote. In a speech given on September 30, Wilson said, "We have made partners of the women in this war. . . . Shall we admit them only to a partnership of suffering and sacrifice and toil and not to a partnership of privilege and right?" Still, the amendment didn't pass that year.

THE WAR AND WOMEN'S SUFFRAGE

When the United States joined World War I in 1917, many Americans rushed to enter the military. With no one else to take over the jobs that the enlisted men left, women stepped in. Their contributions to the war effort and the workforce helped the suffragist cause. Wilson mentioned the war when trying to convince the Senate to pass a suffrage amendment.

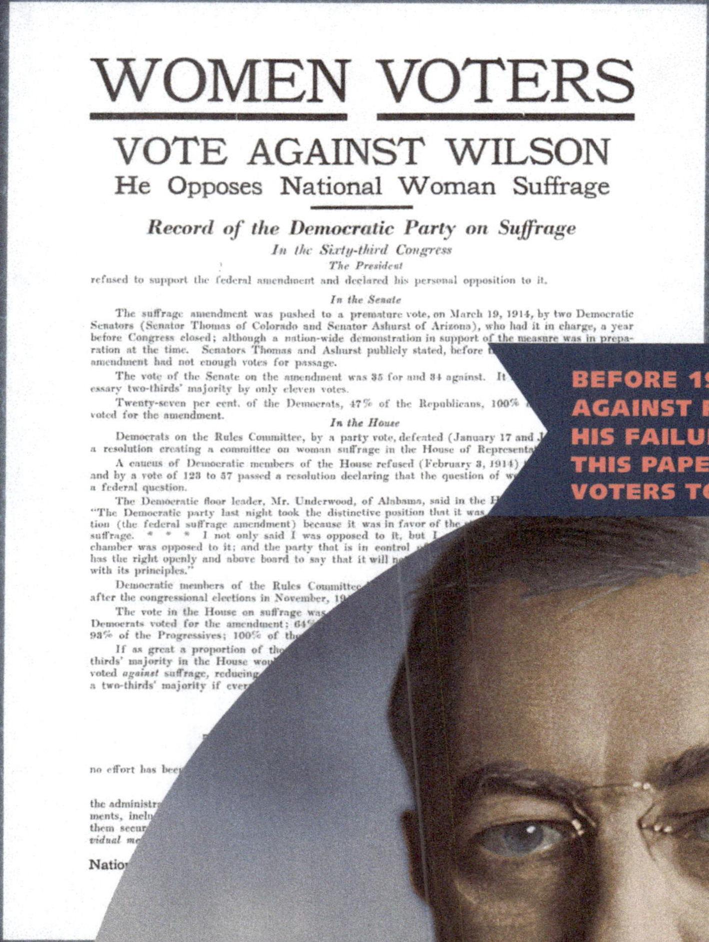

WOMEN VOTERS

VOTE AGAINST WILSON

He Opposes National Woman Suffrage

Record of the Democratic Party on Suffrage

In the Sixty-third Congress

The President

refused to support the federal amendment and declared his personal opposition to it.

In the Senate

The suffrage amendment was pushed to a premature vote, on March 19, 1914, by two Democratic Senators (Senator Thomas of Colorado and Senator Ashurst of Arizona), who had it in charge, a year before Congress closed; although a nation-wide demonstration in support of the measure was in preparation at the time. Senators Thomas and Ashurst publicly stated, before
amendment had not enough votes for passage.

The vote of the Senate on the amendment was 35 for and 34 against. It
essary two-thirds' majority by only eleven votes.

Twenty-seven per cent. of the Democrats, 47% of the Republicans, 100%
voted for the amendment.

In the House

Democrats on the Rules Committee, by a party vote, defeated (January 17 and
a resolution creating a committee on woman suffrage in the House of Representa

A caucus of Democratic members of the House refused (February 3, 1914)
and by a vote of 123 to 57 passed a resolution declaring that the question of w
a federal question.

The Democratic floor leader, Mr. Underwood, of Alabama, said in the H
"The Democratic party last night took the distinctive position that it was
tion (the federal suffrage amendment) because it was in favor of the
suffrage. * * * I not only said I was opposed to it, but I
chamber was opposed to it; and the party that is in control
has the right openly and above board to say that it will n
with its principles."

Democratic members of the Rules Committee
after the congressional elections in November, 19

The vote in the House on suffrage was
Democrats voted for the amendment; 64
93% of the Progressives; 100% of th

If as great a proportion of th
thirds' majority in the House wo
voted _against_ suffrage, reducing
a two-thirds' majority if ever

no effort has bee

the administr
ments, inclu
them secur
vidual me

Natio

BEFORE 1918, MANY SUFFRAGISTS WERE AGAINST PRESIDENT WOODROW WILSON FOR HIS FAILURE TO FIGHT FOR WOMEN'S RIGHTS. THIS PAPER WAS MEANT TO PERSUADE VOTERS TO SUPPORT SOMEONE ELSE.

WOODROW WILSON

THE 19TH AMENDMENT

The U.S. Senate finally approved the suffrage amendment on June 4, 1919. In order for it to become law, the 19th Amendment had to be ratified by at least 36 of the 48 state legislatures. Both the suffragists and their opposition lobbied, or tried to influence, their state representatives to vote in their favor.

Finally, in August 1920, the Tennessee legislature prepared to vote on the amendment. If it approved the amendment, it would be law. At first, there was a tie. Then one representative, 24-year-old Harry Burn, tipped the balance by voting to ratify.

The 19th Amendment states: "The right of citizens of the United States to vote shall not be denied or abridged by the United States or by any State on account of sex." The suffragists had won the long struggle.

THE 19TH AMENDMENT, WHICH BECAME LAW IN 1920, GAVE U.S. WOMEN THE RIGHT TO VOTE.

HEAD TO HEAD

What became the 19th Amendment was first introduced in 1878. California Senator Arlen A. Sargent introduced it at the urging of his friends Elizabeth Cady Stanton and Susan B. Anthony. It was rejected, but a similar bill was introduced every year for 41 years.

RIGHTS TODAY

While there has been progress in achieving equal rights for women over the last 200 years in the United States, people are still working for equality. For example, even though women can hold political office, in 2018, there were three men in office for every woman. Also, for every dollar a man made in 2016, a woman made 80 cents for the same work.

Following the example of suffragists before them, many women are still working for change. In January 2017, for example, women staged a march on Washington, D.C., (and other cities) to **advocate** for many causes. Just like the original women's marches by the suffragists a little more than a hundred years earlier, the march was a reminder of how important it is to have a voice.

WOMEN'S MARCH ON WASHINGTON, 2017

GLOSSARY

activism: Acting strongly in support of or against an issue.

advocate: To support or argue for a cause or policy.

attainable: Able to be accomplished, achieved, or acquired.

calamity: An event that causes great harm and suffering.

corruption: Illegal or dishonest behavior, especially by people in power.

demonstration: An event in which people gather to show how they feel about something.

derogatory: Expressing a low opinion of a person or thing.

heckler: A person who heckles, or interrupts someone rudely and publicly.

inauguration: An event during which a newly elected official moves into a job or position with a formal ceremony.

Parliament: The British lawmaking body.

partisan: Strongly supporting something over something else.

petition: A formal written request to a leader or government regarding a particular cause.

radical: Supporting an extreme or revolutionary part of a political change.

ridicule: To laugh at and make jokes about in a mean way.

tactic: An action that is planned and used to reach a certain goal.

temperance: A movement against alcoholic drinks that took place in the earlier days of the United States.

INDEX

WEBSITES

Due to the changing nature of Internet links, PowerKids Press has developed an online list of websites related to the subject of this book. This site is updated regularly. Please use this link to access the list: www.powerkidslinks.com/oiah/suffragists